THE LIVING FESTIVAL

Jack Priestley — Series

JANIS HANNAFORD

RELIGIOUS AND MORAL EDUCATION PRESS

An Imprint of Arnold-Wheaton

Religious and Moral Education Press
An Imprint of Arnold-Wheaton
Hennock Road, Exeter EX2 8RP

Pergamon Press Ltd
Headington Hill Hall, Oxford OX3 0BW

Pergamon Press Inc.
Maxwell House, Fairview Park, Elmsford, New York 10523

Pergamon Press Canada Ltd
Suite 104, 150 Consumers Road, Willowdale, Ontario M2J 1P9

Pergamon Press (Australia) Pty Ltd
P.O. Box 544, Potts Point, N.S.W. 2011

Pergamon Press GmbH
Hammerweg 6, D-6242 Kronberg, Federal Republic of Germany

Copyright © 1983 Janis Hannaford

All rights reserved. No part of this publication may be reproduced, stored in a retrieval system, or transmitted, in any form or by any means, electronic, electrostatic, magnetic tape, mechanical, photocopying, recording or otherwise, without permission in writing from the publishers.

First published 1983

Printed in Great Britain by A. Wheaton & Co. Ltd, Exeter

ISBN 0 08-029282-8 non net
   0 08-029283-6 net

ACKNOWLEDGEMENTS

The author and publisher wish to thank the following agencies and individuals who kindly provided photographs: British Tourist Authority 27; Ann and Bury Peerless 4, 9, 12, 15, 18; David D. Richardson 11, 25; Ronald Sheridan 20; Victoria and Albert Museum 6.

Cover picture by Ann and Bury Peerless

Contents

Introduction	5
1 The Celebrations	9
2 Stories of Holi	17
3 Symbols and Meanings of Holi	23
Things To Do	28
Material for Teachers	30

Holi revellers

Introduction

If you happened to be visiting India at the beginning of March, during the month called Phalguna, you would be well advised to stay inside on the day after the full moon, especially if you are the sort of person who doesn't like practical jokes. As soon as you walked out into the street you would be soaked to the skin from repeated attacks by groups of children and young men, shrieking, 'Holi hai, Holi hai'. They drench passers-by with buckets of coloured water, or use bicycle pumps to squirt red, yellow and green sprays over everyone within range. Balloons filled with water are hurled over walls and through open windows. Every kind of mischief is played, and handful after handful of multicoloured dust is thrown into the air. It is all very good humoured, and if you enjoy a water fight, there is nothing to stop you joining in and giving back as good as you get. This is Holi, the Festival of Colours, the tumultuous, riotous celebration that ends the Indian year. Everybody is out to have a good time and the three essential elements of the festival are 'rang, ras and rag' – colour, dance and song. The spirit of Holi is foolery and those who are pompous and self-important are shown little mercy at the hands of the merrymakers.

India is a vast country and Holi customs vary, but in most areas huge bonfires are lit. Streets, parks and all public places are crowded with people daubed with colour, clapping, shouting, singing and dancing. They have horns, drums and

An eighteenth century painting showing men and women spraying red water at each other

cymbals and make an unbelievable din. Often all this noise and excitement accompanies a spectacular religious procession swaying its way through the streets with one or more statues held aloft on decorated platforms, surrounded by priests and worshippers.

In many parts of the world the end of winter and the beginning of spring is something that people look forward to. It seems to bring with it feelings of cheerfulness and hope and in many countries, as in India, it is the time at which a new year begins. Although their winters are not as cold as ours, Indians are still glad when they are over. For farmers especially it is an important time. Wheat and barley are ripening and the first harvest of the year will soon begin. In the month of Phalguna, spring is at its height in India, and people seem to catch the exhilarating atmosphere. Although Holi is primarily a Hindu festival, it is a great carnival in which everybody takes part.

The Holi festivities are most popular with young men and boys

1
The Celebrations

Although there are many cinemas in India, and some homes have television sets, these things are found mainly in the towns. In country villages, where most of the population live, cinemas and televisions are not common and it is necessary for people to make their own entertainment. A festival gives everybody a good excuse to enjoy themselves, and people get very involved in organizing the events.

In most villages, various streets or areas have their own *panchayat* or council of residents. There can be a great deal of rivalry between the *panchayats* to put on the largest, most spectacular, and most memorable event. They may arrange for professional entertainers to visit the village, or put on a play or dance-drama of their own. Processions are organized and competitions held to find the best singer or musician in the locality.

Holi is most popular with the young men and boys. From the beginning of the month of Phalguna, they start to build bonfires, collecting fuel wherever they can. They are such keen scavengers that most people take the precaution of removing anything that could be carried away, like garden furniture, from outside their houses. Even so, it is not unknown for a person's fence to disappear! In some parts of India it is customary for the young men to raise funds for the festival by forming groups to perform traditional dances in the streets, similar to English morris dancing.

On the day before the night of the full moon people fast in preparation for the festival, but as dusk falls, a priest lights the bonfire, says a special prayer, and the celebrations begin. Crowds gather to watch as men and boys dance around the flames, even attempting to jump over or through them, often smearing themselves with the ashes. Drums are beaten, horns blown, accompanied by singing, loud shouts and cries.

In areas where the spring crops are ready for harvesting, it is usual to make offerings of those crops to God by placing them on the fire. Barley is roasted in the ashes and then eaten. In some places wheat cakes stuffed with gram (chick-peas) and sugar are thrown into the blaze, and in others, ears of wheat and gram are tied to sugar-cane and dipped into the flames. Coconuts are roasted as they are a symbol of fertility. Some people take home a flaming brand or a little pot of glowing ash in order to light their own fires at home from the Holi fire.

In one of the hill tribes of Nepal, the men dance around the bonfire with drawn swords in memory of their warrior ancestors. They dance so wildly that they fall into a trance as if possessed by the spirits of the dead.

Chir pole and water fights

Throughout most of India the lighting of the bonfire signals a start to the foolery and the throwing of coloured water and powder, but in Nepal it marks the end. There a huge pole called a 'chir' is erected in a prominent place, decorated with strips of cloth, a week before the full moon. With the installation of the chir pole, the fun begins and continues for eight days with all the pranks associated with Holi. On the day of the full moon, at a time when the astrologers' calculations have shown that the omens are good, the pole is lowered and carried away to the prepared bonfire. People snatch wildly at the rags because they are believed to be good luck charms.

Elsewhere, the fights with water and powder begin in earnest the morning after the fire. Crowds surge through the streets of the towns and villages, and small groups break off to visit their friends and relatives to exchange Holi greetings and

Hindus in England celebrate Holi by burning coconuts on a bonfire

Holi crowds surge through the streets of an Indian town

be offered refreshments. At midday they return to their own homes for a special meal. Some people follow a custom of eating only dairy foods on this day, but others consider that the Holi meal should be a real feast.

It sometimes happens that the lively and noisy behaviour in the streets gets a bit out of hand. Tempers flare and fights start. Then the police have to be called in to restore order. More dignified Indians rather look down on such behaviour and hold their celebrations among their own family, indoors or privately in the courtyards of their homes. Many Indian women will not go out during the height of the festivities because of this unruly behaviour.

In the State of Uttar Pradesh, the acknowledged champions of colour throwing take part in a huge procession. Mounted on carts they have to try to defend their position against well-armed groups in the streets. It takes a strong nerve and nimble footwork to avoid getting knocked off the platform by

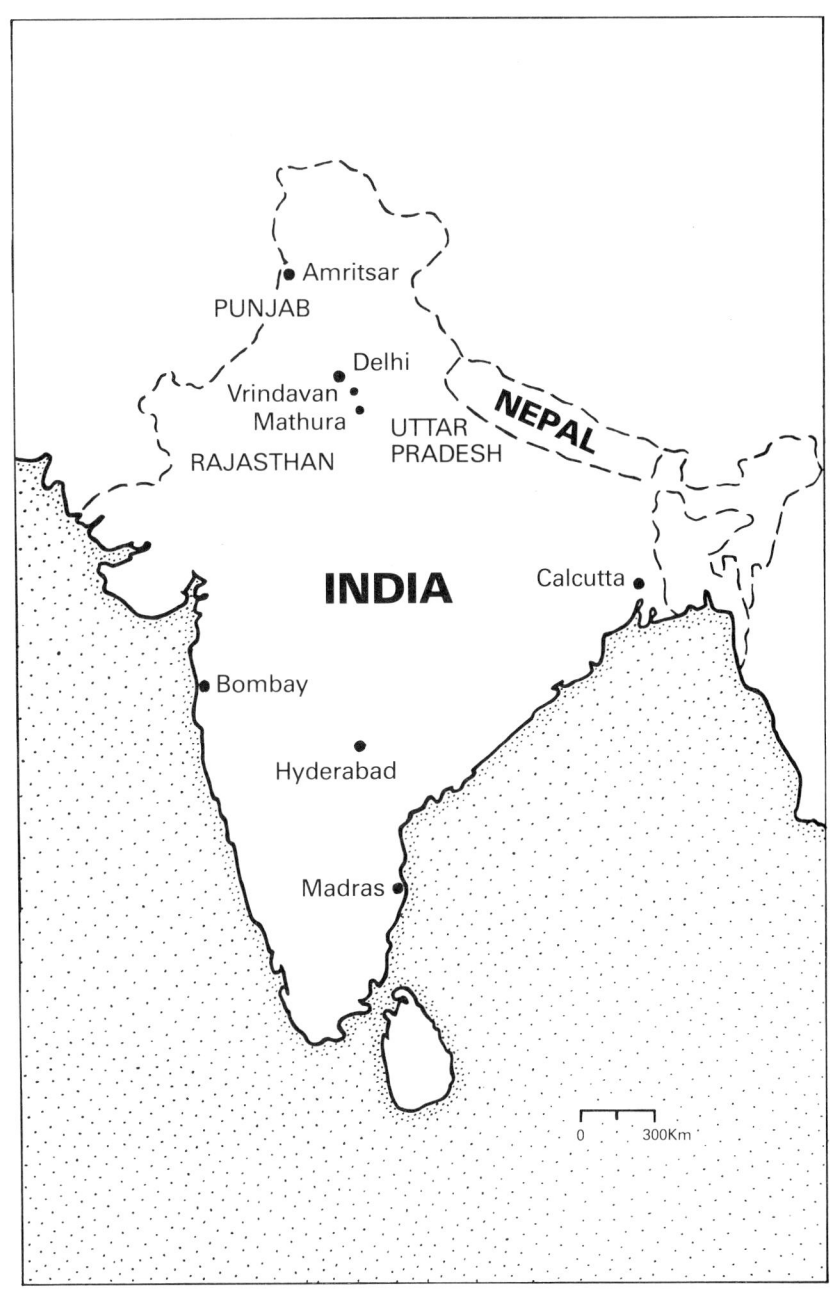

an accurately aimed jet of spray. These carts are followed by others carrying singers and dancers, and the one that ends the procession is a beautifully decorated setting for the statues of the gods. Worship and veneration of the gods is a central part of all the parades, pageants and dramatic presentations during Holi, as it is at all other times in India.

Not far from Delhi, in the north-west of India, an event is held which always attracts a huge crowd. The women of one village have a mock fight with the men of another. The women are armed with long bamboo poles with which they attempt to hit their opponents on the head and shoulders. The men dodge in and out of the onlookers trying to fend off the blows with leather shields and stag horns. Occasionally blood is drawn, but the whole thing is conducted with a lot of hilarity. If the women seem to be getting tired and slowing down, the men taunt and insult them until they can bear it no longer and return to the attack.

The power of dance
In the evening when the excitement of the day dies down, people change into clean clothes. They may assemble in a park or public place to eat together and gossip to the accompaniment of a play, singing, or local folk-dances. Throughout India the power of dance to tell a story is much appreciated and loved. It is one of the most popular ways in which to watch the stories of the gods being told.

Different areas have varying styles of dancing. One of the best known is part of the celebrations in and around the town of Mathura. Called the 'Ras Lila', it is a dance in honour of the early life of the god Krishna. Another custom in this region is the setting up of flower-decorated swings to recall the suspended cradle of the baby Krishna.

Fairs, and even circuses, are often a part of festival celebrations. In the Punjab, Holi fairs are enormous and go on for many days. They can attract up to ten thousand people.

Although a Hindu festival, Holi is generally enjoyed by Indians of other faiths as well – they cannot resist the Holi

Folk dances are an important part of Holi celebrations

madness and fun. One of the best things about Holi is the way in which it breaks down barriers. Personal differences are forgotten, people patch up quarrels, restore friendships and pay or forgive debts. For a few days there is no brooding over the past or worrying about the future. Rich and poor, high and low, young and old join in the excitement to welcome the spring with all the hope and joy the season deserves.

2

Stories of Holi

The people who live in India follow many faiths, but by far the largest number are Hindus. Hinduism is one of the world's oldest religions and amongst the most complex. The beliefs and practices are not clearly laid down, but vary quite considerably from place to place. Although Hindus do believe in one almighty spirit whom they call Bhagvan (or Brahman), they also believe that God is in everything and everywhere. He is seen in all sorts of different ways and is worshipped in many different images. All over India you will find temples and shrines to gods and goddesses all with their own names and unique characters. Individuals or families may be devoted to a certain god or goddess, or to a number of them.

The story of Prahlad

Although Holi is celebrated in some form or another all over India, there are a variety of reasons given for the festival in different parts of the country. One of the most widespread traditions associates the festival with a young boy called Prahlad, a prince in the north-east of India, renowned for being holy and devout. His father, King Hiranya-kasipu, was as evil as Prahlad was good. He issued a decree that throughout his kingdom no one should worship any god, only the king himself. Prahlad, who revered the god Vishnu, refused to obey this command. King Hiranya-kasipu was furious that opposition to his will should come from within his

A woman stops to offer milk to the god of a roadside shrine. The village milkman looks on

own family. He was prepared to do anything to force his son to give up his religion.

First he ordered the boy to be tied to an iron pillar and beaten, but that did not make him change his mind. Then the king put Prahlad in a walled yard with a maddened elephant. Far from trampling him to death, the elephant became quiet and peaceful when the young prince walked towards it reciting the names of the gods. Just below Hiranya-kasipu's palace was a deep pool. The king ruled that his son should be thrown headlong into it from a high, rocky cliff above. Once again Prahlad survived the ordeal. Legend has it that a mark that can be seen on the rocks above this pool is his footprint, and many pilgrims still visit the site of this event, which is in the Jhansi district of India.

Thwarted, the king turned for help to one of his other children, his daughter Holika, a sorceress. She had all kinds of magical powers including the ability to walk through fire without being burned. Giving instructions for a huge pyre to be built, Holika waited until it was burning fiercely, then seized Prahlad and jumped into the very centre of the blaze dragging the boy with her. Scream after scream chilled the watchers. Holika had not known that her spells worked only when she entered the flames alone. Taking her brother with her made the magic useless and she was utterly destroyed. Prahlad, who had once again trusted in God to save him, walked unharmed from the fire. King Hiranya-kasipu was so convinced by this demonstration of the strength of Prahlad's faith that he repented. This was the last time he ever tried to kill his son or force him to change his belief.

Another version of the narrative says that the god Vishnu, to whom Prahlad had prayed throughout all the tortures he had endured, appeared in the form of a lion and tore the wicked king to pieces.

In areas where this story is told, the Holi bonfires are a reminder of the death of Holika and celebrate the triumph of good over evil. Sometimes an effigy of the sorceress is burnt on top of the bonfire.

The custom of making a great deal of noise during the festival is said to go back to another tale about Holika. She was held in such fear by the people that she forced them to provide her with a child a day to eat. Then a wise man told the mothers and children to gather together at a certain spot and, when Holika came along, to start shouting insults at her, screaming as loud as they could. The women scared Holika so much that she never bothered them again.

The story of Kamadeva

In the south of India there are bonfires at Holi, but there they recall the burning of Kamadeva, the love god. Although not a demon like Holika, Kama was a mischievous and thoughtless spirit. In spring he roamed the woods and villages searching out his victims. Once found he would shoot them in the heart with an arrow made of flowers, making them fall hopelessly in love with the first person they saw. One day Kama came across the great god Siva, deep in meditation in a forest clearing. The

Siva, Brahma and Vishnu

impudent spirit thought it would be amusing to cause the mighty Siva to feel the pangs of passion but, as he raised his bow, Siva turned and with one glare reduced Kama to ashes.

When Rati, Kama's wife heard what had happened her grief was overwhelming. With great courage she went to Siva and begged him to restore her husband to life. Eventually her perseverance was rewarded. Siva took pity on her and told her that her husband would be reborn, as love is reborn, not just once, but time after time, only she would never be able to see him. Many of the songs traditionally sung at this time of year are about Rati's sadness at the fate of her husband Kama.

The story of Krishna and Kamsa

Around Mathura, in northern India, where it is said the Holi festival originally began, the celebrations centre around the figure of the popular god Krishna, worshipped by many Hindus. Krishna is said to have been born in this part of India in order to destroy a tyrant called Kamsa. Hundreds of stories are told about the adventures of Krishna as a young man growing up in a village called Vrindavan.

One such tale, especially remembered at Holi, concerns Krishna as a baby. King Kamsa was told by a fortune-teller that he had reason to fear Krishna. Kamsa decided to kill the child immediately, but first he had to find him. He sent a witch called Putana around the countryside to suckle all the male infants she came across and feed them her poisoned milk. When she arrived at Vrindavan village she could not find Krishna, but despite being so young, he recognized her to be a fiendish spirit who appeared in human form. Instead of taking her milk he sucked out all Putana's blood and so put an end to her.

The story of Sambat and Holika

The first day of the month after Phalguna is the Hindu New Year's Day, and far older than any of the other legends is the mythological tale that links Holi with the death of the Hindu year. The god of the year was called Sambat, and he had a sister called Holika. Such was his sister's loyalty, that when Sambat died, Holika insisted on being burnt on his funeral pyre. Through her devotion and sacrifice, Sambat was restored to life.

It is not unusual for festivals, in all parts of the world, to have widely varying stories told to explain their origins. Especially in India, a vast country, where people of many beliefs and languages live, it is not surprising that such stories should be so different. However, it is interesting to see that many of the Holi stories contain similar themes: bonfires and funeral pyres, death and rebirth, and the name Holika is common to many tales.

3
Symbols and Meanings of Holi

It is thought that the celebration of Holi goes back to the early history of India. Holi was probably an ancient harvest festival celebrated long before the spread of Hinduism.

The time of year at which it occurs and the ceremonies performed give clues to the origin of Holi, linking it to similar festivals in other countries. Wherever in the world man began to farm, he celebrated the changing of the seasons and the time of harvest. In the West we can buy the same type of food all the year round and it is difficult for us to imagine the joy the arrival of spring once brought; crops begin to grow again, animals produce young. Spring, with its promise of new life, is a natural time for celebration.

Such an important time often marks the beginning of the New Year and the end of winter. Holi celebrates the passing of the Old Year which, for farmers and those living close to the land, is a turning-point – when the barrenness of winter gives way to the birth of spring. In many countries New Year's Day falls in March or April, not in January, as ours does.

Of course, people involved in trades and professions other than farming see their year ending at other times. In the book on another Indian festival in this series, *Divali*, we find the New Year being celebrated in November. This festival is connected with traders, not farmers, and their year is a 'financial year'. In Britain the financial year begins in April. Schools and colleges work to an 'academic year' which, in

Britain, starts in September and ends in July. When teachers talk about 'next year' they usually mean after the summer holidays, not after 1 January.

Spring festivals

All springtime celebrations have similar characteristics and, although they have changed, it is still possible to recognize some primitive rituals. Perhaps the lighting of fires is the most common. Fire is a symbol of the sun and the greater the blaze the more encouragement it was thought to offer the sun to grow hotter and stronger. All the rubbish that had accumulated during the winter was burnt on the fire. As well as having the practical value of cleaning up this also was a symbolic way of showing the destruction of all evil and impurity. It helped to destroy winter and welcome summer. In the West we still have a similar idea in spring cleaning.

Where the festivities marked the end of the year, it was felt that this ceremony also represented the burning of the Old Year and preparation for the New Year in an atmosphere of purity and cleanliness. People often carried this idea through into their own lives, making this a time when they were under an obligation to settle their debts and patch up quarrels. They too could start the New Year cleansed without anything on their consciences.

Other springtime celebrations involve various practices designed to drive away evil spirits believed to cause crops to fail, or prevent fertility in man or animals. Burning an effigy on the fire is often part of the occasion, as is the making of lots of noise. A deafening racket, rude words and insults are believed to be a way of driving off harmful influences, as we saw in the story of the village mothers and Holika. In many places mock battles are fought, probably dramatizing the defeat of evil by good, or winter by summer. Where these survive they have now become re-enactments of historical events or take the form of rough sports. The wearing of costumes and masks also has a connection with confusing or scaring spirits.

The celebration of spring is bound up with thanksgiving for

Preparing the Holi bonfire at the Hindu temple in Coventry. Coconuts and other offerings are thrown into the fire

the fertility of the land, animals and man. As might be expected there is a certain amount of sensuality in the merrymaking. Bawdy songs, earthy humour, vulgar antics and clowning are very much part of springtime revels throughout the world. Men dress as women, and women as men. They caricature and mock the opposite sex. Those who usually hold positions of respect come in for a great deal of mockery and leg-pulling at this time. In the past it sometimes happened that the usual social positions were completely reversed as part of the New Year fun. The most menial servant would be put in charge, and the master would have to do exactly as he was ordered.

In countries with a long history of Christianity, the importance of Easter tended to put an end to the pre-Christian springtime merriment, but echoes survive in some of the festivities that take place before Lent.* In Germany, for instance, the celebration of 'Fastnacht' involves masked dancers, processions, a mock battle, and a 'prince' with a court of fools. In Britain, folk traditions like the Abbots Bromley Horn Dance, the Burry Man, and the Padstow Old Hoss† have features that suggest they arose from a similar background. Once it was the custom in England to give apprentice boys a holiday on Shrove Tuesday and they used the rare opportunity of a day off to indulge in all sorts of wild pranks. They played a very violent form of football through the streets of the towns and villages. The game was then condemned for the hooliganism and vandalism it encouraged but it still survives in a less violent form.

By looking at all these customs and festivals and by comparing them with Holi it is possible to discover similarities. What at first sight is a typically Indian celebration is shown to have links with other beliefs. The study of festivals

*See *Shrove Tuesday* in this series.
†See *May Day* in this series.

such as Holi not only enables us to understand more about India and Hinduism but also shows us how very different cultures are sometimes linked through customs and celebrations.

The Padstow Old Hoss

THINGS TO DO

N.B. The activities listed below cover a very wide range of ability and aptitude. Selection and direction by the teacher is necessary.

1. It is unlikely that parents or teachers will encourage you to have your own Holi celebration with water fights. Why? Which of the following do you think is most true? Are there any others you can think of?

    In India it is much hotter and getting wet through doesn't matter very much.

    India is a fairly poor country and most of the people who throw dye and colour at one another don't have expensive clothes. Poor people can be more carefree than rich people.

    In India, as in Africa and South-East Asia, people are more relaxed than in Europe and America. They can 'let their hair down' more easily and without feeling self-conscious about it.

2. Draw or paint a Holi street scene or write an imaginative account of 'Arriving in Delhi at Holi'.
3. Draw or paint a bonfire scene like the one described in Chapter 1.

4 Turn either the story of Prahlad or the story of Kamadeva into a dance.
5 Write out one of the stories of Chapter 2 in your own words.
6 Find more stories about the Lord Krishna. Tell one of them in your own words and then describe what sort of character the story shows him to be.
7 In most countries New Year comes at the end of one of the four seasons or at the time when the sun begins to return. When do *you* think New Year should be? When do *you* most feel like starting again? Write down which of the following you think ought to be New Year and give at least one good reason. Then put all the others in order of preference giving at least one reason for the last choice on your list.

> The middle of winter
> The end of February
> The Spring Equinox (21 March)
> The beginning of April (the financial year)
> May Day
> Midsummer's Day
> Harvest time
> September (beginning of the school year)
> The end of autumn and before the winter starts
> Advent (four weeks before Christmas and the beginning of the Christian year)

8 Write a poem or an essay on 'The End of Winter'.
9 From other books in this series find out all you can about the festivals of Divali, Mardi Gras (Shrove Tuesday) and May Day and say how they are like and unlike Holi.
10 Why do we have festivals? If people are not very well off should they waste what little money they have on celebrations? Either write answers to these questions giving reasons and using Holi as an example, or have a properly organized class discussion or debate on them.

MATERIAL FOR TEACHERS

Useful addresses

Hindu Centre
39 Grafton Terrace
London NW5

Institute of Indian Culture
44 Castletown Road
London W14 9HE

Ramakrishna Vedanta Centre
Unity House
Blind Lane
Bourne End
Bucks SL8 5LG

Commonwealth Institute
Kensington High Street
London W8

Books to read

Bahree, Patricia. *The Hindu World*. Macdonald, 1982.
Bridger, P. A. *A Hindu Family in Britain*, Revised Edition. Religious and Moral Education Press, 1984.
Butler, P. G. *Life Among the Hindus*. Arnold.
Ewan, John. *Your Hindu Neighbour*. Lutterworth, 1971.
Ions, Veronica. *Myths and Legends of India*. Hamlyn, 1970.
Nivedita, Sister. *Cradle Tales of Hinduism*. Advaita Ashrama, 1975.
Sharpe, E. J. *Hinduism*. Lutterworth, 1971.
Wayland, Gina D. *Rivers of the World – The Ganges*. Silver Burdett, 1978.
Yogeshananda, S. *The Way of the Hindu*. Hulton, 1973.
Zinkin, Taya. *India and Her Neighbours*. O.U.P., 1967.